Supervising Cybercrime Offenders Through Computer-Related Conditions: A Guide for Judges

Stephen E. Vance
Attorney Advisor
Probation and Pretrial Services Office
Administrative Office of the U.S. Courts

Federal Judicial Center
October 2015

This Federal Judicial Center publication was undertaken in furtherance of the Center's statutory mission to develop educational materials for the judicial branch. While the Center regards the content as responsible and valuable, it does not reflect policy or recommendations of the Board of the Federal Judicial Center.

Contents

Acknowledgments

The author would like to thank John Fitzgerald from the Probation and Pretrial Services Office of the Administrative Office of the U.S. Courts and Joe Gergits from the Office of General Counsel of the Administrative Office of the U.S. Courts for their comments and suggestions on earlier versions of this guide. The author would also like to thank Ellen Fielding from the Probation and Pretrial Services Office of the Administrative Office of the U.S. Courts for her editorial assistance.

I. Introduction

Over the past fifteen years, federal district judges have increasingly imposed special conditions of supervised release and probation restricting computer and Internet use in an effort to protect the public from cybercrime, including child pornography offenses. As computers and the Internet have become more ingrained in society, however, justifying conditions that unnecessarily limit their use has become more difficult. Today, computers and the Internet are used for countless educational, professional, expressive, financial, and other purposes. Recognizing this, some courts have turned to narrower conditions to balance the need for reasonable restrictions with the need for reasonable access. These measures include permitting computer and Internet use based on probation officer approval and authorizing the use of hardware or software to filter, monitor, or record computer and Internet data.

This guide provides an overview of the rapidly evolving law on this topic.[1] Section II summarizes the relevant statutory provisions and Sentencing Guidelines policy statements that courts consider when evaluating computer and Internet special conditions. It also reviews Judicial Conference policy concerning the recommendation and execution of special conditions by federal probation officers. Section III summarizes the types of bans and restrictions on computer and Internet access during postconviction supervision that have been upheld or rejected by courts and discusses the most important factors that courts consider in assessing the restrictions. Section IV describes the factors courts consider when evaluating conditions requiring computer filtering or monitoring and discusses other procedural issues related to the imposition and execution of such restrictions.

---

1. For an introduction to cybercrime from the perspective of probation officer supervision, including technical and legal issues and specific case examples, *see* Mark Sherman, *Special Needs Offenders Bulletin* (Federal Judicial Center 2000).

II. General Legal Framework

A. Statutory Principles

Sentencing courts have broad discretion to impose special conditions of postconviction supervision, provided that several requirements are met. First, the condition must be "reasonably related" to the relevant sentencing factors. For supervised release cases, these factors are (1) the nature and circumstances of the offense, (2) the history and characteristics of the defendant, (3) deterrence, (4) protection of the public, or (5) providing needed correctional treatment to the defendant.[2] For probation cases, these factors are the same as in supervised release cases and also include reflecting the seriousness of the offense, promoting respect for the law, and providing just punishment for the offense.[3] It is not necessary for a special condition to be reasonably related to every sentencing factor. Rather, each factor is an independent consideration to be weighed.[4]

Second, the condition must minimize the deprivation of liberty. For supervised release cases, they must involve "no greater deprivation of liberty than is reasonably necessary" for the purposes of deterrence, protection of the public, and providing needed correctional treatment to the defendant.[5] For probation cases, they must "involve only such deprivations of liberty or property as are reasonably necessary" for the purposes of deterrence, protection of the public, providing needed correctional treatment to the defendant, promoting respect for the law, and providing just punishment for the offense.[6] Third, the condition must be "consistent with any pertinent policy statements issued by the Sentencing Commission."[7]

Appellate courts often require individualized explanations for why special conditions are necessary to achieve the statutory goals of sentencing and how they are sufficiently narrowly tailored.[8] The courts also caution sentencing courts not to apply set packages of special conditions to entire classes or categories of defendants (e.g., all "sex offenders").[9] Courts have rejected and remanded special conditions relating to computer and Internet use for failure to conduct the required individualized inquiry and for failure to articulate findings.[10] When sentencing courts do not set forth factual findings to justify special conditions, some appellate courts have neverthe-

---

2. 18 U.S.C. §§ 3583(d)(1), 3553(a)(1), 3553(a)(2)(B)–(D).

3. *Id.* §§ 3563(b) & 3553(a)(1)–(2).

4. United States v. Tang, 781 F.3d 476, 482 (5th Cir. 2013); United States v. Weatherton, 567 F.3d 149, 153 (5th Cir. 2009); United States v. Weber, 451 F.3d 552, 557–58 (9th Cir. 2006); United States v. Zinn, 321 F.3d 1084, 1089 (11th Cir. 2003); United States v. Brown, 235 F.3d 2, 6 (1st Cir. 2000).

5. 18 U.S.C. §§ 3583(d)(2) & 3553(a)(2)(B)–(D).

6. *Id.* §§ 3563(b) & 3553(a)(2).

7. *Id.* § 3583(d)(3).

8. United States v. Murray, 692 F.3d 273 (3d Cir. 2012); United States v. Forde, 664 F.3d 1219, 1222 (8th Cir. 2012); United States v. Miller, 594 F.3d 172, 184 (3d Cir. 2010); United States v. Keller, 366 F. App'x 362, 363 (3d Cir. 2010) (unpublished); United States v. Warren, 186 F.3d 358, 366 (3d Cir. 1999).

9. United States v. Siegel, 753 F.3d 705, 717 (7th Cir. 2014); United States v. Deatherage, 682 F.3d 755, 765 (8th Cir. 2012); United States v. Bender, 566 F.3d 748 (8th Cir. 2009); United States v. Davis, 452 F.3d 991, 995 (8th Cir. 2006).

10. *See, e.g.*, United States v. Dunn, 777 F.3d 1171 (10th Cir. 2015); United States v. Rodríguez-Santana, 554 F. App'x 23 (1st Cir. 2014) (unpublished); United States v. Dotson, 715 F.3d 576 (6th Cir. 2013); United States v. Goodwin, 717 F.3d 511 (7th Cir. 2013); United States v. Malenya, 736 F.3d 554 (D.C. Cir. 2013); United States v. Inman, 666 F.3d 1001 (6th Cir. 2012); United States v. Wiedower, 634 F.3d 490 (8th Cir. 2011); United States v. Mayo, 642 F.3d 628 (8th Cir. 2011); United States v. Lamere, 337 F. App'x 669, 673 (9th Cir. 2009) (unpublished); United States v. Mark, 425 F.3d 505 (8th Cir. 2005).

less affirmed the condition if they can ascertain a viable basis for the condition in the record based on the presentence investigation report and other documents.[11] However, a condition with no basis in the record or with only the most tenuous basis is less likely to be upheld.[12]

B. United States Sentencing Guidelines

If the instant offense of conviction is a sex offense, the Sentencing Guidelines include a special condition of probation and supervised release "limiting the use of a computer or an interactive computer service in cases in which the defendant used such items."[13] Regardless of the offense of conviction, the court may impose a condition of probation or supervised release prohibiting the defendant from engaging in a specified occupation or limiting the terms on which the defendant may do so only if it determines that (1) there was a reasonably direct relationship between the defendant's occupation and the conduct relevant to the offense of conviction, and (2) imposition of such a restriction is reasonably necessary to protect the public because there is reason to believe that, absent such restriction, the defendant will continue to engage in unlawful conduct similar to that for which the defendant was convicted.[14] As discussed in Section III(B)(1), *infra*, some courts have found that restrictions or bans on computer and Internet use violate the Sentencing Guidelines policy statement on occupational restrictions.

C. Judicial Conference Policy

Under Judicial Conference policy, the specific blend of supervision interventions selected by federal probation officers should be the least restrictive necessary to meet the objectives of supervision in the individual case.[15] Probation officers should consider recommending a special condition to the court only if the officer determines that the mandatory and standard conditions do not adequately address the defendant's risks and needs.[16] Officers are to monitor and facilitate compliance with the conditions using a blend of strategies that are sufficient, but not greater than necessary, to meet sentencing purposes and the objectives in each individual case.[17]

When considering special conditions, officers "should avoid presumptions or the use of set packages of conditions for groups of offenders and keep in mind that the purposes vary depending on the type of supervision."[18] Officers "should ask first whether the circumstances in *this* case require such a deprivation of liberty or property to accomplish the relevant sentencing purposes at *this* time."[19] Good supervision is "tailored to the risks, needs, and strengths presented by the individual offender as determined by careful assessment of each case."[20]

For defendants facing lengthy terms of imprisonment, the officer should consider whether the risks and needs present at the time of sentencing will be present when the defendant returns

---

11. United States v. Heckman, 592 F.3d 400, 405 (3d Cir. 2010); United States v. Voelker, 489 F.3d 139, 144 (3d Cir. 2007).

12. *Heckman*, 592 F.3d at 405; United States v. Burroughs, 613 F.3d 233, 244 (D.C. Cir. 2010).

13. U.S.S.G. §§ 5B1.3(d)(7)(b), p.s. & 5D1.3(d)(7)(b), p.s. The term "sex offense" is defined in Application Note 1 of the Commentary to U.S.S.G. § 5D1.2.

14. U.S.S.G. § 5F1.5, p.s.

15. *Guide to Judiciary Policy* ("*Guide*"), vol. 8E, § 620.60(b).

16. *Id.*, vol. 8D, § 530.20.30(a).

17. *Id.*, vol. 8E, § 210(e)(3).

18. *Id.*, vol. 8D, §§ 240(d) & 530.20.30(b).

19. *Id.* §§ 240(d), 530.20.30(b) (emphasis in original).

20. *Id.*, vol. 8E, § 170(a).

to the community.[21] In some cases, it may be appropriate to avoid recommending special conditions until the defendant is preparing to reenter the community from prison.[22] Throughout the ongoing supervision assessment and implementation process, officers recommend the addition, modification, deletion, amelioration, or suspension of conditions.[23] Officers are to re-evaluate the adequacy and applicability of special conditions throughout the term of supervision.[24] It is particularly important to reassess conditions of supervised release when the defendant is released from prison, because personal, family, and community circumstances may have changed considerably since the defendant was sentenced.[25]

---

21. *Id.*, vol. 8D, § 530.20.30(b).
22. *Id.*
23. *Id.*, vol. 8E, § 210(e)(3).
24. *Id.*, vol. 8D, § 240(c).
25. *Id.*

III. Computer and Internet Restrictions

Defendants have challenged a wide variety of conditions restricting computer and Internet use, ranging from absolute bans to more narrow restrictions that allow for limited use. This is "an area of law that requires a fact-specific analysis,"[26] and there are numerous combinations of factors that may determine whether a restriction is affirmed. Moreover, even when courts are faced with the same set of facts, there is, as one court recently observed, "some tension among various courts of appeals' opinions regarding the reasonableness of restrictions on computer use and Internet access. Dichotomies can be discerned."[27]

A discussion of the most important factors considered provides a helpful framework for analyzing the permissibility of conditions. Courts generally examine (1) the scope of the restriction, including whether computer and Internet use is permitted with probation officer approval or for specific purposes such as employment and education; (2) the nature of the defendant's offense history; and (3) the length of the term of supervision.

A. Scope of Restrictions

1. Absolute Bans

One consideration is whether computer and Internet use is prohibited entirely or whether exceptions are permitted based upon approval of the probation office or for legitimate purposes such as employment and education. As discussed in Section III(A)(2), *infra*, courts are significantly more likely to uphold computer and Internet bans when they allow for limited access. Because absolute bans have been upheld in a relatively small number of cases, a description and discussion of those cases is instructive. The Fifth Circuit held in *United States v. Paul*[28] that it was not an abuse of discretion for the district court to impose a three-year ban on possessing or accessing computers or the Internet. The court reasoned that the defendant "used the Internet to initiate and facilitate a pattern of criminal conduct and victimization."[29] Specifically, the defendant used online resources and bulletin boards to inform others about websites featuring child pornography, he solicited individuals for trips to visit children in Mexico, and he told others "how to 'scout' single, dysfunctional parents and gain access to their children."[30] The Fifth Circuit has subsequently emphasized that the broad scope of the absolute ban in *Paul* was upheld in part because of the short duration of the supervised release term.[31]

In *United States v. McDermott*,[32] the Fifth Circuit held that it was not plain error for the district court to impose a condition prohibiting a defendant convicted of possession of child pornography from possessing or having computer and Internet access. The court reasoned that, alt-

---

26. United States v. Heckman, 592 F.3d 400, 405 (3d Cir. 2010); *see also* United States v. Lantz, 443 F. App'x 135, 142 (6th Cir. 2011) (unpublished) ("Because of the fact-specific nature of other cases imposing restrictions on computer and internet access, and the infinite variations on such restrictions, it is difficult to find cases directly on point.").

27. United States v. Miller, 665 F.3d 114, 127 (5th Cir. 2011).

28. 274 F.3d 155 (5th Cir. 2001).

29. *Id.* at 169.

30. *Id.* at 168.

31. *Miller*, 665 F.3d at 131.

32. 133 F. App'x 952 (5th Cir. 2005) (unpublished).

hough the defendant was not convicted for using his computer and the Internet to facilitate contact with a minor, they were the means that he used to exploit children. The court also rejected the defendant's argument that computer and Internet access would be essential to his ability to earn a living as speculative, given that he was 62 years old.

In *United States v. Johnson*,[33] the Second Circuit upheld a condition barring the defendant from "us[ing] or possess[ing] any computer … with online capabilities at any location until … cleared to do so" by the district court.[34] The offense conduct included using the Internet to conduct sexually explicit conversations with minors and to lure several of them to meetings. Johnson admitted to having sex with two minors and was arrested while on his way to have sex with a third.[35] In upholding the absolute ban, the Second Circuit noted that Internet restrictions "may serve several sentencing objectives, chiefly therapy and rehabilitation, as well as the welfare of the community (by keeping an offender away from an instrumentality of his offenses)."[36] The ban in this case "served these sentencing objectives, confronts Johnson with the need to take his treatment seriously, and serves as an external control to predatory Internet behavior, standing in for Johnson's deficient internal controls."[37]

With regard to whether a lesser restriction could have been imposed instead of a complete ban, the court noted that it had on several occasions vacated absolute bans because narrower restrictions were equally suited to achieving sentencing goals. In those cases, which involved downloading and disseminating child pornography, an outright ban was "held to be more restrictive than needed to serve the sentencing goals of rehabilitation and incapacitation because a combination of monitoring and unannounced inspections would exert the control of an Internet ban while allowing an offender access to the Internet for legitimate purposes."[38]

The court distinguished Johnson's case from cases where computer and Internet bans were vacated based on a combination of his personal characteristics and the nature of his past offenses.[39] Johnson was in denial about his risk of reoffending, had not come to terms with what caused him to commit his crimes, had been "less than truthful with his mental health care providers and with probation," and had "acted in a secretive manner concerning his sexual activity."[40] There was also testimony from the treatment provider that Johnson was at a high risk for reoffending.[41] In addition, he was a sophisticated computer user, and the district court found that a person with his skills likely could circumvent the software needed for monitoring.[42]

As to Johnson's offense history, the court reasoned that, in its prior cases rejecting absolute bans, the defendants were convicted of possession and distribution of child pornography, and the likeliest consequence if a less restrictive measure should fail would be that the defendant would download and distribute child pornography.[43] While these are serious offenses, "the direct harm to children was inflicted previously, when the pornographic images were made, and the

---

33. 446 F.3d 272 (2d Cir. 2006).
34. *Id.* at 281.
35. *Id.* at 275.
36. *Id.* at 281.
37. *Id.* at 282.
38. *Id.* (citing United States v. Sofsky, 287 F.3d 122, 126–27 (2d Cir. 2002)). For a discussion of this line of cases, see Section IV, *infra*.
39. *Johnson*, 446 F.3d at 282.
40. *Id.*
41. *Id.*
42. *Id.*
43. *Id.* at 283.

lesser harm caused by trafficking can be largely remedied afterward, by destroying copies of the material and returning the offender to prison."[44] In Johnson's case, however, the likeliest consequence if a less restrictive measure should fail would be that Johnson could use the Internet to locate children and lure them to sexual abuse. The "perfectly obvious ground for distinguishing [Johnson's case] is that here the failure of lesser measures risks direct harm to children that may be devastating and irremediable."[45] While the court affirmed the computer ban in *Johnson*, it stressed that it was "not hold[ing] that an outright ban on Internet use is categorically appropriate for any sex offender whose offense involves use of the Internet."[46] In light of the fact that Internet access has become "virtually indispensable in the modern world of communications and information gathering,"[47] a "careful and sensitive individualized assessment is always required before such a ban is imposed."[48]

The Fifth Circuit in *United States v. Brigham*[49] affirmed a revocation of supervised release for violation of a condition that the defendant "not possess or utilize a computer or internet connection device during the [three-year] term of supervised release."[50] The court explained that, given the defendant's use of a computer and the Internet to post, receive, and store child pornography images, "a limited period of time—while on supervised release and participating in sex offender treatment—of complete prohibition from such a powerful tool, and access to an enormous amount of persons of all ages, is not unreasonable."[51] Moreover, such a condition both "assists with rehabilitation" and "provides an effective test for [the defendant's] progress, dedication, remorse, willingness, and ability to make the changes in his conduct necessary for his successful unsupervised return to society."[52] The Fifth Circuit concluded that "though [the defendant] is correct that computers and the internet have become significant and ordinary components of modern life as we know it, they nevertheless still are not absolutely essential to a functional life outside of prison."[53]

Finally, in *United States v. Tome*,[54] the Eleventh Circuit upheld a one-year Internet ban as a condition of the defendant's second term of supervised release after he violated conditions allowing for limited Internet use during the first supervised release term. Tome's underlying conviction was for possession of child pornography. The conditions during the first supervision term allowed him to use the Internet for authorized employment purposes, but he had to maintain for his probation officer a daily log of all other Internet use, including use for personal reasons.[55]

Tome was arrested for violating numerous conditions of his supervised release, including Internet restrictions. The district court sentenced Tome to 24 months of imprisonment, followed by one year of supervised release, during which year Tome would be prohibited from accessing the Internet. The district court stated that its decision to restrict access entirely during the second supervised release term was based on his admissions of inappropriate use of the Internet while

---

44. *Id.*
45. *Id.*
46. *Id.* at 282, n.2.
47. *Id.*
48. *Id.*
49. 569 F.3d 220 (5th Cir. 2009).
50. *Id.* at 231.
51. *Id.* at 234.
52. *Id.*
53. *Id.*
54. 611 F.3d 1371 (11th Cir. 2010).
55. *Id.*

already on supervised release, specifically, his using the Internet to communicate with sex-offender inmates, to meet women, and for personal reasons.[56]

The Eleventh Circuit held that the year-long Internet ban was reasonably related to multiple factors listed in 18 U.S.C. § 3553(a).[57] The court rejected Tome's contention that his Internet ban was a greater deprivation of liberty than reasonably necessary based on "his unwillingness to conform his behavior to more lenient restrictions" during the first term of supervised release and the lack of showing that his vocational goals or expressive activities would be negatively affected.[58]

2. Qualified Bans

Several courts examining absolute computer and Internet bans have rejected them as overly broad restrictions of liberty even in cases of extremely serious offense conduct such as using the Internet to attempt to have sexual contact with minors.[59] One court has characterized the Fifth Circuit's opinion in *United States v. Paul*, which upheld an absolute ban, as an "outlier."[60] It further noted that "the computer and internet have permeated everyday life in ways that make a restriction on their use far more burdensome than when *Paul* was decided [in 2001]."[61]

Many courts closely scrutinize computer and Internet bans, not only because of their effect on the defendant's liberty but because they may conflict with the goal of rehabilitation by hampering employment and other opportunities.[62] As one court put it, given "the ubiquitous presence of the internet and the all-encompassing nature of the information it contains," and "the extent to which computers have become part of daily life and commerce," it is "hard to imagine how [defendants] could function in modern society" without computer and Internet access.[63]

---

56. *Id.* at 1375.

57. *Id.* at 1377.

58. *Id.*

59. United States v. Mayo, 642 F.3d 628 (8th Cir. 2011); United States v. Russell, 600 F.3d 631, 637 (D.C. Cir. 2010); United States v. Voelker, 489 F.3d 139, 144 (3d Cir. 2007); United States v. Carlson, 47 F. App'x 598 (2d Cir. 2002) (unpublished).

60. United States v. Russell, 600 F.3d 631, 638 (D.C. Cir. 2010). *See also Voelker*, 489 F.3d at 148 ("Only the Court of Appeals for the Fifth Circuit [in *United States v. Paul*] has approved a complete ban on the use of computers in a precedential opinion, and that was limited to three years."); United States v. Feigenbaum, 99 F. App'x 782, 785 (9th Cir. 2004) (unpublished) ("Most other circuit courts that have addressed the issue have either rejected total Internet bans as conditions of supervised release ... or have allowed Internet bans only where the ban can be lifted at the discretion of a probation officer.").

61. *Russell*, 600 F.3d at 638. While the Fifth Circuit has not found the Internet to be so integral to modern life that a district court may not restrict its use, *Paul*, 274 F.3d 155, 169 (5th Cir. 2001), it has more recently observed that "computers and the internet have become significant and ordinary components of modern life as we know it," *Brigham*, 569 F.3d at 234, and that "access to computers and the Internet is essential to functioning in today's society." United States v. Sealed Juvenile, 781 F.3d 747, 756 (5th Cir. 2015). *See also* Art Bowker, The Cybercrime Handbook for Community Corrections: Managing Offender Risk in the 21st Century 9 (2012) ("[A] total ban on all computer and Internet use ... will be harder and harder to support. This is particularly the case when life in modern society is increasingly dependent upon computer and Internet access.").

62. United States v. Wright, 529 F. App'x 553, 558 (6th Cir. 2013) (unpublished); *Russell*, 600 F.3d 631; *Voelker*, 489 F.3d at 148–49.

63. *Voelker,* 489 F.3d at 148. *See also* United States v. Ullmann, 2015 WL 3559221 (10th Cir. 2015) ("[T]he Internet has become more crucial to participation in employment, communication, and civic life. Internet use is necessary for many jobs, is essential to access information ranging from the local news to critical government documents, and is the encouraged medium for filing tax returns, registering to vote, and obtaining various permits and licenses. Accordingly, we ... hold that conditions imposing complete prohibitions on Internet use or use of Internet-capable

Courts are significantly more likely to uphold computer and Internet bans when they allow for limited use based on probation officer approval or for specified legitimate purposes. These types of restrictions, which are commonly imposed in cases where defendants are convicted of child pornography offenses,[64] are often referred to as "qualified," "conditional," or "modifiable" bans. In many cases where qualified bans have been affirmed, the defendant's offense history includes egregious conduct such as completed sex acts with a child or taking substantial steps toward completion of the acts. (For an extensive list of cases upholding these types of bans, *see* Appendix A.)

Rather than prohibiting all use, courts upholding qualified bans reason that defendants may need access to the computer or Internet for purposes such as employment, education, research, communication, and commerce. Furthermore, these courts argue, qualified bans allow for future adjustments to technology developments and provide a reasonable balance between rehabilitative and deterrence goals.[65] When upholding restrictions allowing for use subject to probation officer approval, courts expect that officers will exercise this authority in a reasonable, responsible, and nonarbitrary manner.[66] This is particularly true given the importance of computers and the Internet for reintegration into society.[67] At least one court has clarified that, while bans subject to probation officer approval are appropriate, it is unreasonably restrictive to require prior probation office permission every single time a defendant needs to use a computer or access the Internet, particularly when there is already a separate condition that restricts access to sexually explicit materials.[68]

B. Nature of Defendant's Offense History

Another factor examined by courts considering computer and Internet restrictions is the nature of the defendant's offense history. In particular, courts assess (1) whether defendants have a history of Internet use for illegal purposes and (2) the severity of their instant offense conduct and prior offense history.

---

devices will typically constitute greater deprivations of liberty than reasonably necessary, in violation of § 3583(d)(2).").

64. *Wright*, 529 F. App'x at 557 ("[T]his is a common special condition with respect to individuals convicted of child pornography crimes.").

65. United States v. Love, 593 F.3d 1, 12 (D.C. Cir. 2010); United States v. Walser, 275 F.3d 981, 988 (10th Cir. 2001).

66. *See also* Arthur L. Bowker, *Computer Crime in the 21st Century and Its Effect on the Probation Officer*, 65 Fed. Probation 18, 19 (2001) ("Absent appropriate training and/or court guidance, some probation officers may be inclined to simply deny any access without regard to the particular circumstances of a case. Such blanket denials may not always pass court scrutiny.").

67. United States v. Morais, 670 F.3d 889, 896 (8th Cir. 2012) ("Given the importance of the Internet as a resource, we expect that the probation office will not arbitrarily refuse such approval when it is reasonably requested and when appropriate safeguards are available."); United States v. Love, 593 F.3d 1, 12 (D.C. Cir. 2010) ("We assume the Probation Office will reasonably exercise its discretion by permitting [the defendant] to use the Internet when, and to the extent, the prohibition no longer serves the purposes of his supervised release.").

68. United States v. Sealed Juvenile, 781 F.3d 747, 756 (5th Cir. 2015) ("We must recognize that access to computers and the Internet is essential to functioning in today's society. The Internet is the means by which information is gleaned, and a critical aid to one's education and social development.... We intend this [condition] to allow for oversight of the ... computer and Internet usage, but not with the heavy burden of requiring prior written approval every time [the defendant] must use a computer or access the Internet for school, health, work, recreational, or other salutary purposes.").

1. Nexus Between Offense History and the Internet

Courts are more likely to uphold restrictions when there is a connection between the defendant's offense history and the Internet. For instance, courts have affirmed conditions for a defendant convicted of bank fraud who had a history of fraudulent Internet transactions and a defendant convicted of mail fraud where the fraudulent activity emanated from an Internet business. On the other hand, Internet restrictions have been rejected for defendants convicted of bank larceny, possession of device-making equipment for "skimming," using a computer to make counterfeit $20 bills, contact sex offenses where the defendant had no history of illegal Internet use, and failure to register under the Sex Offender Registration and Notification Act. (For a list of cases upholding or rejecting restrictions based on whether the defendant's offense history involved illegal use of the Internet, *see* Appendix B.)

Courts have also rejected restrictions in cases where no history of computer and Internet abuse is present as being inconsistent with Section 5D1.3(d)(7) of the Sentencing Guidelines, which recommends "[a] condition limiting the use of a computer or an interactive computer service in cases in which the defendant used such items" in committing a sex offense.[69] Finally, because limiting computer and Internet use can affect employment opportunities, some courts have found that restrictions are inconsistent with Section 5F1.5 of the Sentencing Guidelines, which permits a district court to limit the defendant's ability to engage in a specified occupation or business if there is a reasonably direct relationship between the defendant's occupation and the conduct relevant to the offense of conviction.[70]

2. Severity of Offense History

Another factor courts consider when evaluating computer and Internet restrictions is the severity of the defendant's offense history, particularly for sex-related offenses. Courts are more likely to reject restrictions when computers and the Internet are used exclusively for possession of child pornography. (For a list of cases rejecting Internet restrictions due in part to the lack of use of the Internet for conduct beyond the possession of child pornography, *see* Appendix C.)

On the other hand, courts are more likely to uphold conditions when the defendant uses a computer or the Internet for "child pornography plus" cases "involving not merely possession but additional conduct that threatens the welfare of children."[71] For example, courts have approved restrictions when the defendant: (1) facilitated the real-time molestation of a child when he encouraged another person through an online "chat" to have sexual contact with a young girl; (2) used the Internet as a means to develop an illegal sexual relationship with a young girl; (3) solicited sex with a fictitious minor online; (4) used the Internet to meet and develop a relationship with a young girl, which culminated in a sexual relationship; (5) expressed an interest in

---

69. United States v. Smathers, 351 F. App'x 801 (4th Cir. 2009) (unpublished).

70. United States v. Peterson, 248 F.3d 79, 84 (2d Cir. 2001).

71. Cheryl A. Krause & Luke A.E. Pazicky, *An Un-Standard Condition: Restricting Internet Use as a Condition of Supervised Release,* 20 Fed. Sent'g Rep. 201, 202 (2008). *See also* Art Bowker, *An Introduction to the Supervision of the Cybersex Offender,* 68 Fed. Probation 3, 5 (2004) ("Obviously, more restrictive conditions should be considered for offenders who have personally victimized a minor or demonstrated a willingness to do so. For instance, a traveler (offender who travels across state lines to have sex with a minor) poses a different risk than an individual convicted of simple possession of child pornography."); U.S. Sentencing Commission, Federal Offenders Sentenced to Supervised Release 21 (2010) ("[B]ans on Internet access are sometimes upheld ... if the defendant made some use of the Internet to victimize children.").

young boys in an Internet message, triggering a concern he was willing to use the Internet to facilitate victimization; (6) printed out pictures of child pornography that could be used for distribution; (7) posted pictures of child pornography on a file-sharing program accessible to the public; and (8) joined a child pornography website and initiated contact with an undercover law enforcement officer to order a child pornography video. (A list of cases where courts have upheld restrictions based on conduct where the defendant used the Internet for more than possession of child pornography is available at Appendix D.)

While there appears to be some recognition that computer and Internet restrictions may be greater deprivations of liberty than necessary for defendants who possess or receive child pornography, other courts have refused to adopt this approach and have upheld restrictions when the offense conduct involved no more than possession or receipt of child pornography.[72] In one case, the Eighth Circuit declined to construe its prior cases discouraging Internet restrictions in possession and receipt cases as establishing a *per se* rule against such conditions because "[s]uch a *per se* rule would be in tension with [its] cases holding that a district court should fashion conditions of supervised release on an individualized basis in light of the statutory factors ... and not by treating defendants as part of a class that is defined solely by the offense of conviction."[73] The Eighth Circuit upheld a qualified Internet ban in that case because the defendant's possession of child pornography involved conduct more egregious than in its prior possession cases.[74] At the other end of the spectrum, one court has cautioned against computer and Internet restrictions even when a defendant used the Internet for arranging for sexual contact with a person he believed to be a child.[75]

C. Length of the Term of Supervision

Another factor examined by courts when evaluating technology restrictions is the length of the supervision term. Courts have rejected absolute bans for life[76] or for very lengthy periods.[77] One

---

72. United States v. Wright, 529 F. App'x 553 (6th Cir. 2013) (unpublished); United States v. Morais, 670 F.3d 889 (8th Cir. 2012); United States v. Miller, 665 F.3d 114, 131 (5th Cir. 2011); United States v. Lantz, 443 F. App'x 135, 144 (6th Cir. 2011) (unpublished); United States v. Zinn, 321 F.3d 1084 (11th Cir. 2003).

73. United States v. Morais, 670 F.3d 889, 896 (8th Cir. 2012).

74. *Id.* at 879.

75. In *United States v. Malenya*, 736 F.3d 554, 560 (D.C. Cir. 2013), the defendant was convicted of arranging for a sexual contact with a real or fictitious child. The district court imposed a condition prohibiting access to any computer or online service without the prior approval of the probation officer and requiring installation of a computer and Internet monitoring program. The appellate court stated "[i]t is unclear if *any* computer or internet restriction could be justified in Malenya's case, but the condition in its current form is surely a greater deprivation of liberty than is reasonably necessary to achieve the goals referenced in § 3583(d)." *Id.* at 561. Because the district court failed to weigh the burden of the condition on the defendant's liberty against its likely effectiveness, the appellate court vacated the condition and remanded it to the district court to impose the condition in compliance with 18 U.S.C. § 3583(d).

76. United States v. Duke, 2015 WL 3540562, *6 (5th Cir. 2015) ("No circuit court of appeals has ever upheld an absolute, lifetime Internet ban.... While we have approved absolute Internet bans for limited durations of time ... and lifetime Internet restrictions that conditioned Internet usage on probation officer or court approval..., we have not addressed whether absolute bans, imposed for the rest of a defendant's life, are permissible conditions. We conclude that they are not.... [I]t is hard to imagine that such a sweeping, lifetime ban could ever satisfy §3583(d)'s requirement that a condition be narrowly tailored to avoid imposing a greater deprivation than reasonably necessary."); United States v. Heckman, 592 F.3d 400, 405 (3d Cir. 2010); United States v. Voelker, 489 F.3d 139, 146 (3d Cir. 2007).

reason for this is that extensive terms of supervision may become a "poorer fit over time" as technology changes.[78] When lifetime bans are upheld, they are for qualified bans where exceptions are made based on probation officer approval or for employment purposes.[79] In other cases, even qualified bans for life are rejected.[80] Far shorter technology bans (e.g., for five years) have been either upheld or rejected depending on whether the length of supervision falls within the range of time periods previously examined in cases with similar circumstances.[81] In short, while there is "no precise formula for determining what constitutes a reasonable length of time,"[82] courts examine the duration of technology restrictions as one factor.

D. Other Factors Considered by Courts

In addition to the considerations above, courts examine a variety of factors, including the defendant's computer sophistication and potential ability to evade monitoring software, whether the defendant's occupation requires computers, the temporal remoteness of prior sex offenses, and whether there are other restrictive conditions that make computer or Internet limits unnecessary. As discussed in section III(A)(1), in *United States v. Johnson*[83] the Second Circuit upheld an absolute ban on Internet use in part because the defendant's sophisticated computer skills likely would enable him to circumvent monitoring software, allowing him to continue the offense of having sexually explicit conversations with minors and luring minors into having sex with him.[84]

In *United States v. Granger*,[85] the Fourth Circuit upheld a condition that "[t]he defendant shall not possess or use any computer which is connected or has the capacity to be connected to any network," reasoning that the great majority of the defendant's work history involved manual labor, and therefore the computer restriction would not prevent him from earning a living. Similarly, in *United States v. Knight*,[86] the Fifth Circuit held that the trial court did not abuse its discretion in ordering that the defendant, who was convicted of receiving child pornography, could not own or use a computer at home or at work with Internet or e-mail access without permission from his probation officer. The defendant's livelihood was not dependent on his having access to a computer because he had worked for less than a year in a finance-related position, and as a janitor, test scorer, stock clerk, waiter, and bartender.[87] Finally, in *United States v. Angle*,[88] the Seventh Circuit upheld a special condition of supervised release prohibiting the defendant from hav-

---

77. United States v. Russell, 600 F.3d 631, 638 (D.C. Cir. 2010) (overturning a categorical ban on computer use in part due to the lengthy (30 years) period of the ban).

78. *Id.*

79. United States v. Ellis, 720 F.3d 220, 225 (5th Cir. 2013); United States v. Stults, 575 F.3d 834, 837, 855–56 (8th Cir. 2009); United States v. West, 333 F. App'x 494, 495 (11th Cir. 2009) (unpublished); United States v. Dove, 343 F. App'x 428, 431–32 (11th Cir. 2009) (unpublished); United States v. Boston, 494 F.3d 660, 663, 664 (8th Cir. 2007); United States v. Alvarez, 478 F.3d 864, 865 (8th Cir. 2007).

80. United States v. Miller, 594 F.3d 172 (3d Cir. 2010).

81. United States v. Maurer, 639 F.3d 72, 83 (3d Cir. 2011); United States v. McKinney, 324 F. App'x 180 (3d Cir. 2009) (unpublished); United States v. Freeman, 316 F.3d 386, 392 (3d Cir. 2003).

82. *Maurer*, 639 F.3d at 83.

83. 446 F.3d 272 (2d Cir. 2006).

84. *See* U.S. Sentencing Commission, Federal Offenders Sentenced to Supervised Release 21 (2010) ("[B]ans on Internet access are sometimes upheld … if less restrictive prohibitions would not be effective.").

85. 117 F. App'x 247 (4th Cir. 2004) (unpublished).

86. 86 F. App'x 2 (5th Cir. 2003) (unpublished).

87. *Id.* at 4.

88. 598 F.3d 352 (7th Cir. 2010).

ing "personal access to computer Internet services" because "his use of the Internet was not integrally connected to his profession as he was previously employed as a salesman and mechanic."[89]

In *United States v. T.M.*,[90] the Ninth Circuit rejected a condition that the defendant not possess or use a computer with access to any "on-line computer service" at any location (including place of employment) without the prior written approval of the probation officer based on a charge forty years earlier, later dismissed, of a sexual relationship with a minor, and a kidnaping conviction approximately twenty years earlier involving the undressing and nude picture-taking of an eight-year-old girl. The court explained that conditions predicated solely upon twenty-year-old incidents do not promote the goals of public protection and deterrence.[91] Finally, in *United States v. Russell*,[92] the D.C. Circuit rejected an absolute thirty-year ban on computer use, reasoning in part that "[t]he sentence already achieves considerable severity by its thirty-year term and several other conditions," including the requirements that the defendant register as a sex offender in any jurisdiction where he resides and not be in the presence of anyone under the age of eighteen in a private setting without another adult present.[93]

---

89. *Id.* at 361.

90. 330 F.3d 1235 (9th Cir. 2003).

91. *Id.* at 1240. *See also* United States v. Scott, 270 F.3d 632, 636 (8th Cir. 2001) (finding it unreasonable to impose sex offender conditions on the basis of a past conviction for sexual abuse fifteen years earlier); United States v. Kent, 209 F.3d 1073, 1077 (8th Cir. 2000) (finding that an incident of abuse committed thirteen years earlier does not justify supervised release conditions).

92. 600 F.3d 631 (D.C. Cir. 2010).

93. *Id.* at 637.

IV. Computer and Internet Filtering, Monitoring, and Physical Inspections

While some courts have expressed concern regarding computer and Internet bans, they have also stressed that persons on postconviction supervision are not entitled to unlimited access, particularly if more narrowly tailored restrictions can balance the protection of the public with defendant rehabilitation. Appellate courts have frequently vacated absolute and qualified bans and directed lower courts to devise narrower conditions consisting of some combination of remote filtering, remote monitoring, and in-person searches of computers.[94] When sentencing courts have imposed restrictions other than absolute or qualified bans, such as filtering or monitoring, appellate courts have often upheld them as a middle-ground approach to restrict illicit computer and Internet use while allowing access for legitimate purposes.[95]

There is not a significant body of case law to guide courts as they evaluate the reasonableness of conditions authorizing the filtering, monitoring, or inspection of an defendant's computer. This is due to the nascent nature of the technology and to the fact that these conditions frequently go unchallenged by defendants seeking to avoid bans.[96] The existing cases, however, include some helpful guidance concerning (1) the scope and efficacy of the conditions, (2) the most appropriate defendants for these conditions, and (3) the timing and methods for recommending and implementing the conditions.

---

94. United States v. Duke, 2015 WL 3540562 (5th Cir. 2015); United States v. Phillips, 785 F.3d 282 (5th Cir. 2015); United States v. Dotson, 715 F.3d 576 (6th Cir. 2013); United States v. Miller, 594 F.3d 172 (3d Cir. 2010); United States v. Love, 593 F.3d 1, 11 (D.C. Cir. 2010); United States v. Perazza-Mercado, 553 F.3d 65, 73 (1st Cir. 2009); United States v. Mark, 425 F.3d 505 (8th Cir. 2005); United States v. Freeman, 316 F.3d 386, 392 (3d Cir. 2003); United States v. Holm, 326 F.3d 872, 877–78 (7th Cir. 2003); United States v. Scott, 316 F.3d 733, 735 (7th Cir. 2003); United States v. Sofsky, 287 F.3d 122, 127 (2d Cir. 2002); United States v. Crume, 422 F.3d 728, 733 (8th Cir. 2005); United States v. White, 244 F.3d 1199, 1206–07 (10th Cir. 2001).

95. United States v. Deatherage, 682 F.3d 755, 764 (8th Cir. 2012); United States v. Grigsby, 469 F. App'x 589 (9th Cir. 2012) (unpublished); United States v. Dorner, 409 F. App'x 26 (7th Cir. 2011) (unpublished); United States v. Quinzon, 643 F.3d 1266, 1272 (9th Cir. 2011); *see also* Art Bowker, *An Introduction to the Supervision of the Cybersex Offender*, 68 Fed. Probation 3, 5 (2004) ("Monitoring software/hardware, coupled with computer search/seizure, serves as the least intrusive and restrictive method for controlling the risk that may be posed by most cybersex offenders. Offenders are permitted to use a computer and access the Internet, with the clear understanding that their computer activities are being monitored."); Frank E. Correll, Jr., *"You Fall into Scylla in Seeking to Avoid Charybdis": The Second Circuit's Pragmatic Approach to Supervised Release for Sex Offenders*, 49 Wm. & Mary L. Rev. 681, 684 (2007) (referring to computer monitoring as the "pragmatic middle ground" because it allows sentencing courts and probation officers to use technology to avoid the opposing extremes of banning computer and Internet use altogether or not placing any restrictions).

96. United States v. Ullmann, 2015 WL 3559221, *2 (10th Cir. 2015); United States v. Legg, 713 F.3d 1129 (D.C. Cir. 2013) (holding it was not plain error to impose condition allowing random searches of, and installation of monitoring programs on, computer, noting that counsel for defendant conceded that the conditions were "pretty standard in cases like this"); United States v. Heckman, 592 F.3d 400, 408 (3d Cir. 2009) ("[T]here are alternative, less restrictive, means of controlling [the defendant's] post-release behavior, including the computer monitoring condition already imposed by the District Court in this case (and that [the defendant] has not challenged)."); United States v. Mark, 425 F.3d 505, 509 (8th Cir. 2005) ("According to Mark, the district court could have addressed its concerns by ordering him to install filtering software that would block access to sexually-oriented websites and to permit the probation office unannounced access to verify that the software was functioning properly.").

A. Scope and Efficacy: Minimal Intrusiveness and Maximal Effectiveness

In *United States v. Lifshitz*,[97] the court provided perhaps the most thorough legal analysis of computer monitoring conditions. In *Lifshitz*, the defendant pleaded guilty to receiving child pornography over the Internet. The district court imposed a condition of probation that allowed the probation office to "monitor or filter computer use on a regular or random basis" without any individualized suspicion and to make, "upon reasonable suspicion … unannounced examinations of any computer equipment owned or controlled by the defendant."[98]

In addressing whether the condition resulted in a deprivation of liberty greater than reasonably necessary, the court held that the condition must "seek a minimum of intrusiveness coupled with maximal effectiveness."[99] The precise type of monitoring technology is the critical factor when evaluating whether a condition satisfies this standard. According to the court, there was very little information in the record about the kind of monitoring authorized by the condition.[100] The court conducted a brief survey of monitoring technology and stated that there are two principal axes along which monitoring methods can be distinguished. First, some monitoring uses software installed on an individual's personal computer, whereas other monitoring relies on records from the Internet Service Provider (ISP), through whom an account user's requests for information or e-mails are routed.[101] The former type of monitoring might be more conducive to investigating all of a probationer's computer-based activities, including those performed locally without connection to the Internet or any network, whereas the latter would be limited to transmissions mediated by the ISP.[102] Second, some software focuses attention upon specific types of unauthorized materials, whereas other kinds monitor all activities engaged in by the computer user.[103]

Constant inspection of the documents that Lifshitz created on his computer might, as the court put it, "be more like searching his diary or inspecting his closets than it is like the highly targeted diagnosis accomplished by drug testing."[104] By contrast, software that alerted a probation officer only when Lifshitz was engaging in impermissible communications over e-mail or the Internet would "bear much greater resemblance to screening a probationer's urine for particular drugs—as opposed to investigating a sample to ascertain all medical conditions from which the individual suffered or to figure out his or her favorite foods."[105] These types of distinctions, according to the court, may be relevant to determining whether the scope of the monitoring condition's infringement on privacy is commensurate with the special needs of rehabilitation and deterrence.[106]

In addition to the uncertain scope of the condition, it was not clear whether the monitoring would be effective. The court noted that experienced computer users were quite resourceful in circumventing the software employed.[107] It was not obvious from the record that computer

---

97. 369 F.3d 173 (2d Cir. 2004)
98. *Id.* at 177.
99. *Id.* at 186.
100. *Id.* at 190.
101. *Id.*
102. *Id.*
103. *Id.*
104. *Id.* at 192.
105. *Id.*
106. *Id.*
107. *Id.*

monitoring would be immune from such evasion.[108] The court therefore vacated the condition and remanded the case to the district court to evaluate whether the proposed monitoring techniques were sufficiently narrowly tailored and maximally effective compared to less restrictive alternatives such as filtering the electronic data accessed by the defendant.[109]

The appellate court suggested that the district court might wish—through a hearing or other appropriate procedures—to evaluate the scope and efficacy of the methods of computer monitoring or filtering that the probation office intended to employ. If it appeared that filtering was no less effective than monitoring, the court might decide to permit filtering rather than monitoring. If, on the other hand, there were demonstrable advantages to monitoring, the court might instead prefer to ensure that a narrower but still effective condition be imposed, if one was reasonably available.[110] Finally, if at some point in the future the defendant presented clear evidence that less intrusive but still effective methods of controlling his computer use had become technologically available, the court stressed that nothing in its decision would preclude the district court from modifying its order.

According to one legal commentator, this approach places a substantial fact-finding burden on courts and probation officers:

> In the *Lifshitz* ruling, the Second Circuit left it to the district court to determine just what methods of computer monitoring are permissible. This places a heavy burden on the lower courts to review search technologies and find facts regarding their effectiveness in targeting specific types of computer use. *Lifshitz* exacerbates this burden by providing that a probationer could return to the court and request a modification of the supervision conditions upon introduction of a new privacy-enhancing search capability. In addition, each approach to computer monitoring can be circumvented depending on the technical skills of the probationer. As a result, courts must continually revise search approaches depending on the available technology and the characteristics of the probationer.[111]

B. Applicability of Conditions

When considering whether conditions requiring computer and Internet filtering or monitoring are appropriate, courts examine factors similar to those considered for computer and Internet bans (*see* Section III, *supra*). Courts have found, for instance, that filtering and monitoring are more appropriate than bans in cases where defendants did not use the Internet to contact young children.[112] As one court put it, using the Internet for solicitation of children is "more difficult to

---

108. *Id.*

109. *Id.*

110. For example, two ways in which the condition might be more narrowly tailored would be by limiting it to Internet-related activity and e-mail and by implementing monitoring software that searches for particular suspect words and phrases rather than recording all varieties of computer-related activity. This was not to suggest, according to the Second Circuit, that the condition must necessarily be restricted to the monitoring of online conduct. *Id.*

111. Shawna Curphey, *United States v. Lifshitz: Warrantless Computer Monitoring and the Fourth Amendment*, 38 Loy. L.A. L. Rev. 2249, 2262 (2005).

112. United States v. Freeman, 316 F.3d 386, 392 (3d Cir. 2003); United States v. Sofsky, 287 F.3d 122, 126–27 (2d Cir. 2002).

trace [through computer monitoring] than simply using the internet to view pornographic web sites."[113]

Courts are also more likely to affirm these measures in cases where there is a connection between the Internet and the defendant's offense history.[114] Not all courts, however, agree that an Internet nexus is required. Courts have held that a history of Internet abuse is not necessary to impose a monitoring condition when the defendant had a documented history or propensity for sexually deviant or other inappropriate behavior toward minors.[115] Another court has upheld a computer monitoring condition where the defendant had no history of using a computer to commit an offense but used a cell phone to send threatening text messages.[116] Courts also assess the characteristics of the defendant, including whether the nature of the defendant's profession gives him access to children,[117] and the defendant' mental illness and young age.[118]

C. Timing and Methods for Imposing and Executing Conditions

Courts have also discussed procedural and logistical issues concerning the imposition of conditions that remotely monitor or filter computer and Internet use. Some courts have suggested that, where technological considerations prevent specifying at the time of sentencing how a condition is to be implemented following years of imprisonment, a modification of conditions after sentencing or a postponement in imposing conditions should be considered to ensure that they re-

---

113. *Freeman*, 316 F.3d at 392.

114. United States v. Stergios, 659 F.3d 127, 134 (1st Cir. 2011); United States v. Burroughs, 613 F.3d 233, 244 (D.C. Cir. 2010); United States v. Smathers, 351 F. App'x 801, 802 (4th Cir. 2009) (unpublished); United States v. Peterson, 248 F.3d 79, 83 (2d Cir. 2001).

115. United States v. McGee, 559 F. App'x 323, 330 (5th Cir. 2014) (unpublished) (for defendant convicted of failure to register as a sex offender, upholding a condition requiring the installation of filtering software regarding sexually arousing material, reasoning that the condition was reasonably related to public protection from defendant's "very troubling, sexually deviant criminal history," and noting that, while there was no nexus between defendant's offense history and Internet use, the sentencing court found defendant was a "predator" due to his criminal history, including multiple charges for aggravated rape of minors, and the sentencing court justified the condition as "a precaution, purely protective" because of its concern "about the stimulation factor motivating [defendant] for additional types of conduct consistent with child molestation"); United States v. Perazza-Mercado, 553 F.3d 65, 73 (1st Cir. 2009) ("Although the internet did not play a role in the sexual misconduct which was the basis for his conviction, we must also consider Perazza–Mercado's documented propensity for inappropriate behavior towards young girls. The personal characteristics of the defendant, even though they do not reflect any history of computer misuse, could justify a targeted limitation on internet use involving certain kinds of chat rooms or any sites involving children. . . Because of this concern, and the nature of his prior conduct, other conditions of Perazza–Mercado's supervised release forbid him from working with children in a professional capacity and residing or loitering near areas which are frequented by groups of children.... We can imagine, and modern technology permits, an internet prohibition which would essentially replicate these real-world limitations.").

116. United States v. Hayes, 283 F. App'x 589 (9th Cir. 2008) (unpublished) (upholding condition requiring monitoring of defendant's computer and "other electronic devices or media," reasoning that cell phones qualify as "other electronic devices" and that, in light of the defendant's history of threatening and volatile behavior, the district court could have reasonably concluded that allowing the probation officer to inspect and monitor Hayes's personal computer—which, in turn, may deter Hayes from utilizing another viable means of sending threats to his family—was reasonably necessary to achieve deterrence or public protection).

117. United States v. Mangan, 306 F. App'x 758, 760 (3d Cir. 2009) (unpublished) ("We conclude, in light of the record before us, that the basis for each of these conditions of supervised release [including computer monitoring] is patent given ... his status as an educator.").

118. United States v. Sealed Juvenile, 781 F.3d 747, 757 (2015) ("Appellant is a mentally ill juvenile. Given the potential influence of the Internet on his sexual development, ... it is in the interests of deterrence and rehabilitation to monitor his access to technology.").

main both narrowly tailored and effective as technology and other circumstances change.[119] Other courts have taken or suggested an incremental approach where less restrictive measures permitting some degree of Internet access are imposed initially and, if violated, replaced by more restrictive conditions.[120]

Some courts suggest that a ban that delimits computer and Internet use based on probation officer approval may be a more effective way to implement remote filtering and monitoring software because it provides the officer with the flexibility to adjust to rapidly changing technology, while a stand-alone monitoring condition may become outdated, ineffective, or overly burdensome after lengthy periods of incarceration and supervision.[121] Courts delegating to officers the authority to determine how best to implement monitoring and filtering conditions emphasize the officer's continuing duty to make adjustments with changing technology to ensure maximal effectiveness and minimal intrusiveness.[122] Other courts, however, caution that district courts should adopt precise rules rather than open-ended delegations to avoid arbitrary execution of the condition.[123]

Many courts that impose computer-monitoring conditions intend that the monitoring be done on a regular or random basis without individual showings of reasonable suspicion. If the court intends that regular or random computer monitoring be done without an individual demonstration of reasonable suspicion, it may be prudent to make that intention clear in the special condition of supervision.[124] One court has upheld on plain error review a condition requiring that

---

119. United States v. Siegel, 753 F.3d 705, 717 (7th Cir. 2014) (recommending as a "best practice" for sentencing judges imposing conditions of supervised release that they "[r]equire that on the even of his release from prison, the defendant attend a brief hearing before the sentencing judge (or his successor) ... to consider whether to modify one or more of the conditions in light of changed circumstances"); United States v. Kent, 554 F. App'x 611 (9th Cir. 2014) (unpublished) (noting that if technology has changed by the time the defendant is released from prison, and he believes that the probation office has not met its continuing obligation to ensure not only the efficacy of the computer monitoring methods, but also that they remain reasonably tailored so as not to be unnecessarily intrusive, he may seek relief from the district court at that time); United States v. Quinzon, 643 F.3d 1266, 1273 (9th Cir. 2011) ("[A]s new technologies emerge or circumstances otherwise change, either party is free to request that the court modify the condition of supervised release ... In situations like this one, where technological considerations prevent specifying in detail years in advance how a condition is to be effectuated, district courts should be flexible in revisiting conditions imposed to ensure they remain tailored and effective."); United States v. Balon, 384 F.3d 38, 47 (2d Cir. 2004) (stating that changing technology "is an appropriate factor to authorize a modification of supervised release conditions under Section 3583(e)."); United States v. Lifshitz, 369 F.3d 173, 193, n.11 (2d Cir. 2004) ("Because Lifshitz is being sentenced to probation, it seems necessary to determine, at this time, the conditions of that probation and to base that determination, in the first instance, on the state of technology and other practical constraints as they currently exist. Were this, however, a case involving supervised release, or if there were any reasons why the commencement of the defendant's term of probation would be substantially delayed, it might well be prudent for the district court to postpone the determination of the supervised release or probation conditions until an appropriate later time, when the district court's decision could be based on then-existing technological and other considerations.").

120. United States v. Freeman, 316 F.3d 386, 392 (3d Cir. 2003) ("[I]f Freeman does not abide by more limited conditions of release permitting benign internet use, it might be appropriate to ban all use.").

121. United States v. Kent, 554 F. App'x 611 (9th Cir. 2014) (unpublished); United States v. Miller, 665 F.3d 114, 124 (5th Cir. 2011); United States v. Quinzon, 643 F.3d 1266, 1273 (9th Cir. 2011); United States v. Love, 593 F.3d 1, 11 (D.C. Cir. 2010).

122. United States v. Quinzon, 643 F.3d 1266, 1273 (9th Cir. 2011).

123. United States v. Scott, 316 F.3d 733, 735 (7th Cir. 2003).

124. David N. Adair, Jr., *Looking at the Law*, 65 Fed. Probation 66, 67 (2001) ("Given the lack of certainty in the requirement of reasonable suspicion, and the fact that the use of [computer monitoring] software is less intrusive than a full-blown computer search, it is understandable that some courts will want monitoring to be done without a necessity for reasonable suspicion.... [S]uch monitoring should be conducted pursuant to specific court authoriza-

the defendant install filtering software on his personal computers to monitor and block websites containing illegal child pornography and allowing the probation office "unannounced access" to his personal computers "to verify that the filtering software is functional."[125] The court held that the condition was reasonably related to the defendant's offense history involving computer use and did not violate the defendant's Fourth Amendment rights.[126] It noted that the sentencing judge "reasonably found that the monitoring program will 'ensure compliance' with the other conditions, most notably the condition prohibiting [the defendant] from receiving, transmitting, or viewing illegal pornography."[127] Furthermore, it reasoned that "[t] he deterrent effect of filtering software—and unannounced checks to determine the software remains functional—is apparent."[128]

Another court has upheld on plain error review a condition requiring that the defendant "consent to ... periodic unannounced examinations of his computer, hardware, and software which may include retrieval and copying of all data from his computer [and] removal of such equipment, if necessary, for the purpose of conducting a more thorough inspection."[129] It reasoned in part that these conditions are "reasonably necessary, as an additional safeguard to supplement the [computer-monitoring software], to ensure that the [defendant] does not access prohibited materials and to check whether he does access them."[130]

---

tion in the form of a special condition that permits the use of the particular software. And, if it is the intent of the court that the results will be monitored by a probation officer on a regular or random basis, the condition should specifically so state.").

125. United States v. Kappes, 782 F.3d 828, 857 (7th Cir. 2015).

126. *Id.*

127. *Id.*

128. *Id.*

129. United States v. Sealed Juvenile, 781 F.3d 747, 757 (5th Cir. 2015).

130 *Id.*

V. Conclusion

In recent years, sentencing courts have increasingly imposed special conditions of supervised release and probation restricting computer and Internet use. Appellate courts appear to examine similar factors when considering these conditions, though there are differences among circuits depending on the specific facts and circumstances in each case. At the same time, the case law is still evolving to address rapidly changing technology. A significant challenge has been to apply legal standards to complex and evolving forms of technology used to commit cyber crime, to monitor computer and Internet use, or to evade monitoring of computer and Internet use.

Appendix A: Cases Upholding Qualified Bans

United States v. Rath, 2015 WL 3559160 (5th Cir. 2015) (for defendant convicted of abusive sexual contact with a minor, upholding conditions prohibiting access to any computer capable of Internet access, reasoning in part that defendant may use a computer for school and work as long as the computer is not capable of Internet access)

United States v. Sealed Juvenile, 781 F.3d 747, 756 (5th Cir. 2015) (upholding condition that the defendant not possess or use a computer with access to any "on-line computer service" without the prior written approval of the probation office, but construing the condition to not require the defendant to seek written permission "every single time he must use a computer or access the Internet")

United States v. Ullman, 2015 WL 3559221 (10th Cir. 2015) (upholding condition restricting Internet access without probation office approval, noting that all Internet access is not prohibited and that devices without Internet access, such as gaming systems, are not restricted)

United States v. Smith, 564 F. App'x 200, 208 (6th Cir. 2014) (unpublished) (upholding condition limiting computer and Internet access except with probation officer approval, reasoning in part that the court "reasonably lessened the impact of the restrictions by stressing that Smith's probation officer would have the flexibility to approve Smith's use of cell phones and computers")

United States v. Sullivan, 588 F. App'x 631 (9th Cir. 2014) (unpublished) (for defendant convicted of making a threatening communication in violation of 18 U.S.C. § 875(c) through use of electronic communications, including the Internet, upholding computer restriction in part because the restriction was not absolute and permitted access when approved by the probation office)

United States v. Valdoquin, 586 F. App'x 513 (11th Cir. 2014) (unpublished) (upholding condition limiting computer use in part because defendant retained the right to use a computer with access to the Internet based on the district court's approval)

United States v. Ellis, 720 F.3d 220, 224 (5th Cir. 2013) (upholding a condition requiring the defendant to receive prior approval from the court before "possess[ing], hav[ing] access to, or utiliz[ing] a computer or internet connection device including, but not limited to Xbox, PlayStation, Nintendo, or similar device")

United States v. Wright, 529 F. App'x 553 (6th Cir. 2013) (unpublished) (for defendant who possessed and distributed child pornography, upholding a ban on Internet use except with probation officer approval because the ban was not absolute and was therefore reasonable and consistent with the sentencing objectives of 18 U.S.C. § 3553 and 18 U.S.C. § 3583(d))

United States v. Atias, 518 F. App'x 843, 846-47 (11th Cir. 2013) (unpublished) (upholding computer and Internet restrictions as a condition of supervised release where defendant, who was convicted of receipt of child pornography, could still "petition the court for approval to use either a computer or the internet")

United States v. Legg, 713 F.3d 1129 (D.C. Cir. 2013) (where defendant was convicted of persuading a person to travel in interstate commerce to engage in criminal sexual activity, holding it was not plain error to impose conditions forbidding the defendant from possessing or using a computer or any online service without prior approval of the probation office, and requiring him to identify all computer systems and Internet-capable devices to which he would have access, and to allow random searches of, and installation of monitoring programs on, those devices, noting that counsel for defendant conceded that the conditions were "pretty standard in cases like this")

United States v. Hilliker, 469 F. App'x 386, 387 (5th Cir. 2012) (unpublished) (holding it was not plain error to "den[y] all access to computers, the internet, cameras, photographic equipment, and other electronic equipment without the permission of his probation officer" for a defendant with a fugitive background who was a "predator" and who had repeatedly engaged in direct physical contact with minor children and who admitted that Internet pornography was a factor in clouding his judgment regarding the propriety of touching or fondling young girls in public places)

United States v. Borders, 489 F. App'x 858, 863 (6th Cir. 2012) (unpublished) (upholding condition for defendant convicted of possession of child pornography that he "shall not utilize a computer unless for legal, outside employment or for an express class assignment in an accredited educational institution and with the approval of the probation officer")

United States v. Lewis, 565 F. App'x 490 (6th Cir. 2012) (unpublished) (finding no abuse of discretion for ban on use of a computer with access to any "on-line service" or other forms of wireless communication without the prior approval of the probation officer)

United States v. Black, 670 F.3d 877, 883 (8th Cir. 2012) (district court did not plainly err by prohibiting defendant from accessing Internet without prior officer approval because defendant was "not just a passive possessor of child pornography" but rather had accessed the child pornography through a Limewire file-sharing program, and because defendant may still access the Internet with the permission of the probation office)

United States v. Morais, 670 F.3d 889, 897 (8th Cir. 2012) ("The special condition at issue here is not a complete ban on use of the Internet. With prior approval of the probation office, Morais may access the Internet for legitimate purposes of research, communication, and commerce.")

United States v. Muhlenbruch, 682 F.3d 1096 (8th Cir. 2012) (holding it was not an abuse of discretion to prohibit defendant, who was convicted of possession and receipt of child pornography, from possessing a computer or accessing the Internet without prior approval of the probation officer)

United States v. Munjak, 669 F.3d 906 (8th Cir. 2012) (upholding a ban on Internet access without probation officer approval for defendant convicted of possession of child pornography who possessed images of child pornography on a computer and who distributed them by using a peer-to-peer file-sharing program, reasoning that the ban was reasonably necessary to further the purposes of sentencing, including deterrence and protection of the public)

United States v. Accardi, 669 F.3d 340, 347 (D.C. Cir. 2012) (upholding on plain error review a ban on "possess[ion] or use [of] a computer that has access to any online computer service at any location, including [the defendant's] employment, without the prior approval of the probation office")

United States v. Maurer, 639 F.3d 72, 83 (3d Cir. 2011) (upholding qualified Internet ban, reasoning that the scope of the restriction was sufficiently narrow because, rather than restrict all computer use, the court limited only the defendant's access to the Internet, with exceptions to be provided by the probation office)

United States v. Demers, 634 F.3d 982, 983 (8th Cir. 2011) (upholding condition banning the defendant from having access to an Internet-connected computer or accessing the Internet from any location without first demonstrating a "justified reason" for that access and obtaining the approval of the probation officer, where the defendant had a prior history of sexual abuse and possession of child pornography)

United States v. Fletcher, 435 F. App'x 578 (8th Cir. 2011) (unpublished) (upholding on plain error review the special condition of supervised release prohibiting defendant from having Internet access at his residence, and from having—without prior approval by the probation office and a justified reason—access to an Internet-connected computer or other device with Internet capabilities or access to the Internet from any location)

United States v. Mayo, 642 F.3d 628 (8th Cir. 2011) (upholding condition restricting access to the Internet unless it is necessary for employment purposes and the probation officer approves it)

United States v. Phillips, 370 F. App'x 610, 620 (6th Cir. 2010) (unpublished) (upholding special condition prohibiting defendant "from owning, using or possessing a computer or any other internet-capable electronic device without the written permission of his probation officer," reasoning that the restrictions were not overly restrictive because they did not ban all computer and Internet use and they were reasonably related to protection of the public and rehabilitation)

United States v. Angle, 598 F.3d 352 (7th Cir. 2010) (for defendant convicted of possession of child pornography, attempted receipt of child pornography, and attempt to entice a minor, via Internet and telephone, to engage in sexually prohibited activity, upholding a condition prohibiting defendant from having "personal access to computer Internet services," reasoning in part that the ban was not a complete ban because it disallowed only "personal" access)

United States v. Durham, 618 F.3d 921, 944 (8th Cir. 2010) (district court did not abuse its discretion in imposing a restriction on Internet access when the restriction did not amount to a total ban, reasoning in part that the condition "must be treated as merely a partial deprivation of Durham's interest in having unfettered access to the Internet")

United States v. Koch, 625 F.3d 470, 482 (8th Cir. 2010) (upholding qualified ban where defendant was permitted to use a computer and the Internet with prior approval from a probation officer "who will have the guidance of our case law, which recognizes the importance of computers and internet access for education, employment, and communication, when considering [defendant's] requests")

United States v. Thielemann, 575 F.3d 265, 278 (3d Cir 2009) (emphasizing the relatively limited coverage of the ban, noting that the defendant could seek permission from the probation officer to use the Internet and that he could "own or use a *personal* computer as long as it is not connected to the Internet; thus he is allowed to use word processing programs and other benign software")

United States v. Loflin, 318 F. App'x 212 (4th Cir. 2009) (unpublished) (for defendant convicted of traveling in interstate commerce to engage in a sexual act with a juvenile and transportation of a minor in interstate commerce with intent to engage in criminal sexual activity, holding it was not an abuse of discretion to impose a special condition limiting use of a computer without probation officer approval)

United States v. Bender, 566 F.3d 748 (8th Cir. 2009) (holding it was not an abuse of discretion to prohibit possession or use of a computer or any device with access to any online computer service without probation officer approval)

United States v. Moran, 573 F.3d 1132, 1141 (11th Cir. 2009) (for a defendant convicted of felon in possession of a firearm, holding that the court did not abuse its discretion by imposing special condition restricting defendant's access to the Internet without probation officer approval, reasoning that, although the Internet provides valuable resources for information and communication, it also serves as a dangerous forum in which a defendant can access child pornography and communicate with potential victims, and the defendant may still use the Internet for valid purposes by obtaining permission)

United States v. Beeman, 280 F. App'x 616, 619 (2008) (upholding conditions restricting Internet access without probation office approval and allowing the probation office to monitor defendant's computer-based activities in part because they did not involve an unreasonable deprivation of liberty because defendant may use computers and access the Internet with the permission of the probation office)

United States v. Brimm, 302 F. App'x 588 (9th Cir. 2008) (unpublished) (holding the district court did not abuse its discretion when it imposed a special condition of supervised release that prohibited the defendant from using a computer with access to any online services, except for use with his employment and after the approval of the probation officer, and rejecting the contention that the condition constituted an unwarranted occupational restriction because it did not interfere with the defendant's employment)

United States v. Goddard, 537 F.3d 1087, 1090 (9th Cir. 2008) (finding that condition requiring that defendant "use only those computers and computer-related devices, screen user names, passwords, email accounts, and internet service providers (ISPs) as approved by the Probation

Officer" where "computers and computer-related devices include, but are not limited to, personal computers, personal data assistants (PDAs), internet appliances, electronic games, and cellular telephones, as well as their peripheral equipment, that can access, or can be modified to access, the internet, electronic bulletin boards, other computers, or similar media" was not an abuse of discretion)

United States v. Nisely, 172 F. App'x 713 (9th Cir. 2006) (unpublished) (for defendant convicted of use of a facility of interstate commerce to attempt to induce a minor to engage in criminal sexual activity, holding that prohibition against Internet access without probation officer permission did not involve greater deprivation of liberty than reasonably necessary)

United States v. Sullivan, 451 F.3d 884, 887 (D.C. Cir. 2006) (upholding on plain error review the condition that the defendant "shall not possess or use a computer that has access to any 'on-line computer service' at any location, including his place of employment, without the prior written approval of the Probation Office," where "on-line computer service" included, but was not limited to, "any Internet service provider, bulletin board system, or any other public or private computer network")

United States v. Antelope, 395 F.3d 1128, 1142 (9th Cir. 2005) (affirming the imposition of a condition prohibiting defendant from "possess[ing] or us[ing] a computer with access to any 'on-line computer service' at any location (including employment) without the prior written approval of the probation department")

United States v. Vinson, 147 F. App'x 763, 775 (10th Cir. 2005) (unpublished) (for defendant convicted of subscribing to a false tax return, wire fraud, and mail fraud, upholding a condition prohibiting the defendant from using any Internet service without first receiving written permission from his probation officer, noting its assumption that, the officer "will implement this condition without a greater intrusion of [defendant's] liberty than is necessary")

United States v. Landry, 116 F. App'x 403, 407 (3d Cir. 2004) (unpublished) (upholding on plain error review a restriction where the defendant was not prohibited from using stand-alone computers without Internet access and where Internet access was permitted upon probation officer approval)

United States v. Harding, 57 F. App'x 506, 507 (3d Cir. 2003) (unpublished) (upholding a condition that the defendant shall "not possess or use a computer with access to any online computer service at any location, including employment, without prior approval of the probation officer")

United States v. Knight, 86 F. App'x 2 (5th Cir. 2003) (unpublished) (holding that the trial court did not abuse its discretion in ordering that the defendant, who was convicted of receiving child pornography, could not own or use a computer at home or at work with Internet or e-mail access without permission from his probation officer and that any computer he used must be blocked from accessing child pornography Internet sites, reasoning in part that the claim that the defendant did not victimize anyone with his computer is without merit and in contradiction to his guilty plea for receiving images of child pornography on his home computer)

United States v. Crandon, 173 F.3d 122, 125, 128 (3d Cir.1999) (upholding a condition that directed the defendant not to "possess, procure, purchase[,] or otherwise obtain access to any form of computer network, bulletin board, Internet, or exchange format involving computers unless specifically approved by the United States Probation Office," reasoning that the restrictions are permissible because the special condition is narrowly tailored and is directly related to deterrence and protecting the public)

United States v. Fields, 324 F.3d 1025, 1027 (8th Cir. 2003) (ban on use of a computer without probation officer permission did not constitute abuse of discretion where the offense of conviction involved running a child pornography website for profit)

United States v. Ristine, 335 F.3d 692 (8th Cir. 2003) (finding no plain error where the district court barred the defendant from having Internet service at his residence and where other Internet access was permissible upon probation office approval)

United States v. Rearden, 349 F.3d 608, 620 (9th Cir. 2003) ("We recognize the importance of the Internet for information and communication, but we disagree that the condition is plainly impermissible in Rearden's case as it leaves open the possibility of appropriate access…The condition does not plainly involve a greater deprivation of liberty than is reasonably necessary for the purpose because it is not absolute; rather, it allows for approval of appropriate online access by the Probation Office.")

United States v. Taylor, 338 F.3d 1280 (11th Cir. 2003) (finding that condition prohibiting defendant from using or possessing a computer with Internet access without probation officer approval was not an abuse of discretion in part because, if defendant had a legitimate need to use a computer, the district court's order authorized his probation officer to allow that use)

United States v. Zinn, 321 F.3d 1084, 1092 (11th Cir. 2003) ("We realize the Internet has become an important resource for information, communication, commerce, and other legitimate uses, all of which may be potentially limited to [defendant] as a result of our decision. Nevertheless,…the restriction in this case is not overly broad in that [defendant] may still use the Internet for valid purposes by obtaining his probation officer's prior permission.")

United States v. Suggs, 50 F. App'x 208, 211 (6th Cir. 2002) (unpublished) (upholding a condition of supervised release in a fraud case that prohibited defendant from having access to a personal computer except for employment purposes)

United States v. Walser, 275 F.3d 981, 988 (10th Cir. 2001) (upholding prohibition where defendant could use the Internet with permission of the probation office)

United States v. Crandon, 173 F.3d 122 (3d Cir. 1999) (upholding a three-year ban prohibiting the defendant from using any "computer network, bulletin board, Internet, or exchange format involving computers" without permission from the probation office)

Appendix B: Cases Upholding or Rejecting Bans Based on Nexus Between Offense History and Internet Use

United States v. Rath, 2015 WL 3559160 (5th Cir. 2015) (for defendant convicted of abusive sexual contact with a minor, upholding conditions prohibiting access to any computer capable of Internet access and requiring defendant to consent to installation of computer-monitoring software, reasoning in part that, although the facts of the instant conviction did not involve a computer, defendant used Internet access—specifically, email and instant messaging—to groom a subsequent victim over an extended period of time in developing a relationship that culminated in illegal sexual intercourse)

United States v. Fernandez, 776 F.3d 344, 348, (5th Cir. 2015) (for defendant convicted of failing to register as a sex offender under the Sex Offender Registration and Notification Act, holding that court abused its discretion in imposing a special condition requiring the installation of computer-monitoring software, when neither the defendant's failure-to-register offense nor his criminal history had any connection to computer use or the Internet, and noting that "[i]n the absence of evidence to the contrary, the court's general concerns about recidivism or that [defendant] would use a computer to perpetrate future sex-crimes are insufficient to justify the imposition of an otherwise unrelated software-installation special condition")

United States v. Ramos, 763 F.3d 45 (1st Cir. 2014) (for defendant convicted of aiding and abetting in the production of child pornography, vacating prohibition on any access to internet, without permission from probation officer, reasoning that the district court did not cite evidence that defendant used a computer or the Internet in any way in connection with the offense, nor did it identify past impermissible uses that justified generally barring him from using a computer or the Internet, and leaving in place a more narrowly tailored monitoring and filtering condition that was not challenged by defendant)

United States v. Baker, 755 F.3d 515, 525 (7th Cir. 2014) (for defendant convicted of failing to register as a sex offender under the Sex Offender Registration Act, rejecting condition requiring participation in the probation office's computer and Internet monitoring program because the conviction "in no way require[d], or [was] facilitated through, the use of a computer")

United States v. Sullivan, 588 F. App'x 631 (9th Cir. 2014) (unpublished) (for defendant convicted of making a threatening communication in violation of 18 U.S.C. § 875(c) through use of electronic communications, including the Internet, upholding computer restriction in part because the use of a computer and the Internet was essential to the commission of the crime)

United States v. Valdoquin, 586 F. App'x 513 (11th Cir. 2014) (unpublished) (upholding condition limiting computer use in part because defendant downloaded approximately 400 images of child pornography, including material that depicted sadistic or masochistic conduct, approximately 200 of which involved children between the ages of four and eleven and others that involved minors who were at least twelve years old)

United States v. Tang, 718 F.3d 476, 483 (5th Cir. 2013) (for a defendant convicted of failure to register as a sex offender, holding it was an abuse of discretion to impose a ban on Internet use without probation officer permission because the ban was not reasonably related to the statutory sentencing factors, reasoning that the defendant had never committed an offense over the Internet and his prior conviction for assault with intent to commit sexual abuse did not involve any use of a computer or the finding of the minor victim online, and that restricting the defendant's access to a computer had the potential to stifle any educational and vocational training)

United States v. Doyle, 711 F.3d 729 (2013) (for defendant convicted of failure to register as a sex offender, vacating qualified Internet ban, reasoning that the record did not show why ban related to rehabilitating defendant or protecting the public)

United States v. Maxwell, 483 F. App'x 233 (6th Cir. 2012) (unpublished) (vacating condition banning defendant from possessing an Internet-capable device without probation officer approval, reasoning that there was no history of using a computer or the Internet to facilitate prior offenses, and remanding to sentencing court for further exposition of how condition was reasonably related to defendant's history and characteristics)

United States v. Stergios, 659 F.3d 127 (1st Cir. 2011) (upholding special condition for defendant convicted of bank fraud imposing a ban—except when approved by the supervising officer—on Internet access where the defendant relied heavily on the Internet to perpetrate his frauds by opening banking accounts and conducting money transfers and where the defendant had a history of fraudulent Internet transactions)

United States v. Springston, 650 F.3d 1153, 1156 (8th Cir. 2011) (for defendant convicted of failing to register as a sex offender, holding that district court abused its discretion by imposing special condition prohibiting Internet access without probation officer approval because the record was devoid of evidence that the defendant had ever used a computer for any purpose related to the offense)

United States v. Laureys, 653 F.3d 27 (D.C. Cir. 2011) (for defendant convicted of attempted enticement of a minor and traveling across state lines with intent to engage in illicit sexual conduct, upholding condition requiring defendant to log all Internet addresses he accessed and to disclose computer restrictions to potential employers, reasoning that defendant used the internet to facilitate criminal sexual conduct with minors)

United States v. Heckman, 592 F.3d 400 (3d Cir. 2010) (a condition banning Internet use was plain error because of the length (lifetime) and coverage (no exceptions for approved use) of the ban, and, although defendant's criminal history was extensive, he had never been convicted of criminal behavior that involved the use of the Internet)

United States v. Keller, 366 F. App'x 362 (3d Cir. 2010) (unpublished) (upholding special condition banning defendant from using the Internet to create "business websites" because it was directly related to the criminal conduct underlying Keller's mail fraud conviction, to wit: mail fraud emanating from an Internet candy business)

United States v. Perazza–Mercado, 553 F.3d 65, 74 (1st Cir. 2009) (overturning as overbroad a total ban on the defendant's residential Internet use where the defendant had "no history of impermissible Internet use and the Internet was not an instrumentality of the offense of conviction" and remanding to the district court so that, in light of a variety of technological options at its disposal, it might devise a more limited restriction)

United States v. Smathers, 351 F. App'x 801 (4th Cir. 2009) (unpublished) (striking down on plain error review a special condition forbidding the defendant from "possess[ing] or us[ing] a personal computer or any other means to access any 'on-line computer service' at any location (including employment) without the prior approval of the probation officer [including] any Internet service provider, bulletin board system, or any other public or private computer network," reasoning that there was no history of using the computer or the Internet to obtain or disseminate child pornography and therefore the condition was not related to the factors in 18 U.S.C. 3553(a) nor was it in line with the Sentencing Commission's policy statement in Section 5D1.3(d)(7) recommending "[a] condition limiting the use of a computer or an interactive computer service in cases in which the defendant used such items" in committing a sex offense)

United States v. Barsumyan, 517 F.3d 1154, 1160 (9th Cir. 2008) (rejecting on plain error review prohibition on "access[ing] or possess[ing] any computer or computer-related devices in any manner, or for any purpose" for a defendant convicted of possession of device-making equipment in part because, while a computer was required to download the credit card numbers that a skimming device skimmed, defendant was an intermediary who told Secret Service agents that he knew two individuals who would be able to produce cards from the numbers provided on the skimmer, and there was no indication that defendant was going to be the one to do the downloading)

United States v. Beeman, 280 F. App'x 616, 619 (2008) (unpublished) (upholding conditions restricting Internet access without probation office approval and allowing the probation office to monitor defendant's computer-based activities in part because they were reasonably related to the goals of protecting the public and deterring defendant from repeating his criminal conduct, which involved using a computer to view and download child pornography)

United States v. Sales, 476 F.3d 732, 736 (9th Cir. 2007) (rejecting condition forbidding access to computers and computer-related devices that could access or be modified to access the Internet, electronic bulletin boards, and other computers, or similar media where the defendant had been convicted of using his personal computer, scanner, and printer to make counterfeit $20 bills, and his offense in no way involved or relied upon the Internet, reasoning that "[t]he breadth of [the condition] is not reasonably related to the nature and circumstances of Sales's counterfeiting offense or Sales's history and characteristics," and that "the condition "results in a far greater deprivation of Sales's liberty than is reasonably necessary to prevent recidivism, protect the public, or promote any form of rehabilitation")

United States v. Peterson, 248 F.3d 79, 81 (2d Cir. 2001) (for defendant convicted of bank larceny with a prior state incest conviction, rejecting condition imposing restrictions on computer ownership and Internet access where there was no indication that defendant's past incest offense had any connection to computers or to the Internet)

Appendix C: Cases Rejecting Bans Based on
Lack of Conduct Beyond Possession or Receipt of Child Pornography

United States v. Phillips, 785 F.3d 282 (8th Cir. 2015) (vacating condition banning defendant from accessing the Internet without written approval, which was premised in part on defendant's possession of adult pornography, reasoning that because possession of child pornography may not necessarily justify a ban, a court exceeds its discretion by imposing a ban for possession of adult pornography)

United States v. Wiedower, 634 F.3d 490 (8th Cir. 2011) (vacating a condition banning the use of *any* computer, whether connected to the Internet or not, without prior approval of the probation officer where the defendant did not use a computer to do more than possess and receive child pornography (he was convicted of possessing two images and three short videos of child pornography), and remanding to the district court to create a more narrowly tailored ban)

United States v. Miller, 594 F.3d 172, 176 (3d Cir. 2010) (striking down a lifetime supervised release condition that prevented Miller from using without prior written approval a computer with Internet access, reasoning that Miller's case involved receipt and possession of child pornography, whereas other cases upholding Internet bans involved the active solicitation of sexual contact with minors)

United States v. Heckman, 592 F.3d 400, 405 (3d Cir. 2009) (rejecting on plain error review a special condition where the defendant was "prohibited from access to any Internet service provider, bulletin board system, or any other public or private computer network" for the remainder of his life—without exception due not only to the length and scope of the condition but to the fact that the defendant had no history of using the Internet either to lure a minor into direct sexual activity or to entice another to exploit a child)

United States v. Voelker, 489 F.3d at 144, 146 (3d Cir. 2007) (rejecting as overbroad a lifetime condition prohibiting the defendant from "accessing any computer equipment or any 'on-line' computer service at any location, including employment or education. This includes, but is not limited to, any internet service provider, bulletin board system, or any other public or private computer network," and reasoning in part that the defendant "did not use his computer equipment to seek out minors nor did he attempt to set up any meetings with minors over the internet")

United States v. Crume, 422 F.3d 728, 733 (8th Cir. 2005) (striking down as not reasonably necessary a ban prohibiting defendant from using a computer or the Internet without the prior approval of the probation office, because despite the defendant's "grievous" history of sexual misconduct, there was no evidence he had ever used his computer "for anything beyond simply possessing child pornography," and concluding that the district court could "impose a more narrowly-tailored restriction on Mr. Crume's computer use through a prohibition on accessing certain categories of websites and Internet content and can sufficiently ensure his compliance with this condition through some combination of random searches and software that filters objectionable material")

United States v. Mark, 425 F.3d 505, 510 (8th Cir. 2005) (vacating the special conditions of supervised release prohibiting access to any online computer programs, and prohibiting the use or possession of a computer with Internet access, where the criminal conduct involved simple possession of child pornography, and remanding to the district court to consider less restrictive alternatives such as filtering software and unannounced computer inspections)

Appendix D: Cases Upholding Bans Based on Conduct Beyond Possession or Receipt of Child Pornography

United States v. Black, 670 F.3d 877 (8th Cir. 2012) (district court did not plainly err by prohibiting defendant from accessing the Internet without prior officer approval because defendant was "not just a passive possessor of child pornography" but rather had accessed the child pornography through a Limewire file-sharing program)

United States v. Muhlenbruch, 682 F.3d 1096, 1105 (8th Cir. 2012) (holding it was not an abuse of discretion to prohibit defendant from possessing a computer or accessing the Internet without prior approval of the probation officer, reasoning in part that the defendant used his computer for something "beyond simply possessing child pornography" by saving images of child pornography, including images of prepubescent minors engaged in sadistic or masochistic violence, to a disk—a readily transferable medium)

United States v. Maurer, 639 F.3d 72, 84 (3d Cir. 2011) (for defendant convicted of possession of child pornography, holding that the district court did not plainly err in imposing an Internet ban, reasoning in part that "[t]he scope of the restriction [was] … sufficiently narrow" because "[r]ather than restricting all computer use, the District Court limited only Maurer's access to the internet, with exceptions to be provided by the Probation Office")

United States v. Demers, 634 F.3d 982 (8th Cir. 2011) (for defendant convicted of possession of child pornography, upholding on plain error review a condition forbidding him from accessing an Internet-connected computer or from accessing the Internet from any location without prior approval by the probation office, reasoning in part that Demers was arrested at a public library after having printed images of child pornography, which could very well have been done for the purpose of distributing those images)

United States v. Angle, 598 F.3d 352 (7th Cir. 2010) (for defendant convicted of possession of child pornography, attempted receipt of child pornography, and attempt to entice a minor, via Internet and telephone, to engage in sexually prohibited activity, upholding a condition prohibiting defendant from having "personal access to computer Internet services," reasoning in part that the defendant was convicted of more than possession of child pornography)

United States v. Durham, 618 F.3d 921, 944 (8th Cir. 2010) (district court did not abuse its discretion when the restriction did not amount to a total ban, reasoning that "there is no real doubt that restricting [the defendant's] access to the Internet is reasonably related to the nature and circumstances of the offense—which, at a minimum, involved using [a file-sharing program] to acquire a large collection of child pornography")

United States v. Love, 593 F.3d 1, 511 (D.C. Cir. 2010) (upholding condition that the defendant "shall not possess or use a computer that has access to any online computer service at any location, including his place of employment, without the prior written approval of the Probation Office," reasoning that the defendant not only distributed child pornography but also solicited sex with a fictitious young girl online)

United States v. McKinney, 324 F. App'x 180 (3d Cir. 2009) (unpublished) (upholding condition that defendant could not possess or use a computer with Internet access or possess a device capable of transmitting child pornography without the approval of the probation officer, reasoning in part that defendant's conduct involved mechanisms of Internet communications rather than solely accessing child pornography websites)

United States v. Thielemann, 575 F.3d 265, 267 (3d Cir. 2009) (upholding a ten-year, conditional ban on Internet access as narrowly tailored and closely related to the goals of deterrence and public protection where the defendant was actively involved not only in distributing child pornography but also in using the Internet to facilitate, entice, and encourage the real-time molestation of a child when he encouraged another person through an online "chat" to have sexual contact with a young girl)

United States v. Bender, 566 F.3d 748 (8th Cir. 2009) (holding it was not an abuse of discretion to prohibit possession or use of a computer or any device with access to any online computer service without probation officer approval, reasoning in part that the defendant arranged online to meet a woman for sexual relations, and pursued a sexual relationship despite discovering that she was a minor)

United States v. Alvarez, 478 F.3d 864, 868 (8th Cir. 2007) (affirming on plain error review a qualified condition prohibiting residential Internet access where defendant admitted that he had a problem with self-control and that every prior attempt to curtail his access to prohibited material had been unsuccessful, where the defendant's statements and actions could be interpreted to suggest that online material provided him with actionable ideas, and where defendant's employment history (which included work as a stocker at a store) did not indicate that he had a particular day-to-day vocational need for Internet access)

United States v. Boston, 494 F.3d 660, 668 (8th Cir. 2007) (holding that the special condition prohibiting Boston from accessing or possessing a computer without written approval of his probation officer did not constitute an abuse of discretion because it was not absolute and because evidence was presented that Boston had used a computer to print out images of child pornography, which could easily have been done for the purpose of transferring them to others)

United States v. Antelope, 395 F.3d 1128, 1142 (9th Cir. 2005) (affirming the imposition of a condition prohibiting defendant from "possess[ing] or us[ing] a computer with access to any 'online computer service' at any location (including employment) without the prior written approval of the probation department," where defendant joined an Internet site advertising "Preteen Nude Sex Pics" and started corresponding with and ordered a child pornography video from an undercover law enforcement agent, and where the use of the Internet was "essential" to the crime and where the crime was "one step on a path towards more serious transgressions")

United States v. Landry, 116 F. App'x 403, 407 (3d Cir. 2004) (unpublished) (upholding on plain error review a restriction where the defendant was not prohibited from using stand-alone computers without Internet access and where Internet access was permitted upon probation officer approval, reasoning that the defendant was not acting as a "simple 'consumer'" of child pornography, but as "someone directly involved in the exploitation of children" because "he not only traded in the pornographic material, but in fact created some of it")

United States v. Fields, 324 F.3d 1025, 1027 (8th Cir. 2003) (ban on use of computer without probation officer permission did not constitute abuse of discretion where the offense of conviction involved running a child pornography website for profit, which was more serious than a possessory offense because it exploited young girls by making materials available to child predators, and the defendant pointed to no specific negative impact on his educational or vocational training that would result from the condition)

United States v. Ristine, 335 F.3d 692, 696 (8th Cir. 2003) (finding no plain error where the district court barred the defendant from having Internet service at his residence, where the defendant "more than merely possessed images of child pornography-he exchanged the images with other Internet users, and he attempted to arrange sexual relations with underage girls")

United States v. Taylor, 338 F.3d 1280 (11th Cir. 2003) (finding that condition prohibiting defendant from using or possessing a computer with Internet access without probation officer approval was not an abuse of discretion where defendant engaged in a series of harassing and threatening activities, including posting a message on an Internet bulletin board successfully encouraging men to call a woman's twelve-year-old daughter in order to engage in sexual activities)

United States v. Paul, 274 F.3d 155, 169 (5th Cir. 2001) (affirming a total ban on defendant's Internet and computer use where he had previously used the Internet to "encourage exploitation of children by seeking out" other pedophiles and advising them on how to locate potential child victims)

United States v. Crandon, 173 F.3d 122, 145 (3d Cir. 1999) (upholding a three-year ban prohibiting the defendant from using any "computer network, bulletin board, Internet, or exchange format involving computers" without permission from the probation office as narrowly tailored and related to deterrence and public protection for a defendant's use of the Internet to contact a minor, initiate a personal encounter and subsequently engage in sexual activities, photographically record the activities, and receive the images through interstate commerce)